YOUR KNOWLEDGE HAS VALUE

- We will publish your bachelor's and master's thesis, essays and papers

- Your own eBook and book - sold worldwide in all relevant shops

- Earn money with each sale

Upload your text at www.GRIN.com
and publish for free

Bibliographic information published by the German National Library:

The German National Library lists this publication in the National Bibliography;
detailed bibliographic data are available on the Internet at http://dnb.dnb.de .

This book is copyright material and must not be copied, reproduced, transferred, distributed, leased, licensed or publicly performed or used in any way except as specifically permitted in writing by the publishers, as allowed under the terms and conditions under which it was purchased or as strictly permitted by applicable copyright law. Any unauthorized distribution or use of this text may be a direct infringement of the author s and publisher s rights and those responsible may be liable in law accordingly.

Imprint:

Copyright © 2014 GRIN Verlag
Print and binding: Books on Demand GmbH, Norderstedt Germany
ISBN: 9783668672703

This book at GRIN:

https://www.grin.com/document/416858

Felix G.

The Ukraine Conflict. A Short History Outline

GRIN Verlag

GRIN - Your knowledge has value

Since its foundation in 1998, GRIN has specialized in publishing academic texts by students, college teachers and other academics as e-book and printed book. The website www.grin.com is an ideal platform for presenting term papers, final papers, scientific essays, dissertations and specialist books.

Visit us on the internet:

http://www.grin.com/

http://www.facebook.com/grincom

http://www.twitter.com/grin_com

28 October 2014

Conflict Map
The Ukraine Conflict
Background: Description of the Country and History Outline

Fig. A: Map of Ukraine before the Ukraine Crisis (Your-Vector-Maps.com, 2012)

Ukraine is located in Eastern Europe between Moldova, Romania, Hungary, Slovakia, Poland and Belarus in the West and Russia and the Black Sea in the East. The unitary state of Ukraine has 24 oblasts (administrative units), one autonomous republic (Crimea), two municipalities (Kiev and Sevastopol) and a population of 45,6 million people (78% of these are Ukrainians, 17% are Russian, 0,6% Belarusians and 0,5% are Crimean Tatars) (Auswärtiges Amt, 2014). The capital and biggest city is Kiev with 2,7 million inhabitants. Ukraine's economy gained a Gross Domestic Product (official exchange rate) of $175,5 billion in 2013 and had a growth rate of 0,4% but underwent a hard economic period with a contraction of 15% in 2009 (CIA, 2014). Ukraine is dependant on Russia for energy supply (gas).

Ukraine gained independence with the dissolution of the Union of Soviet Socialist Republics (USSR) in 1991. Corruption and state control stood democracy, civil rights, privatisation and economic reformation in the way and led to a peaceful "Orange Revolution" in 2004. Following this revolution Victor Yushchenko, a reformist, was elected for president. However, disagreements in the reformists party led rival Viktor Yanukovych to gain political power. He was elected for Prime Minister in 2006 and then for president in 2010. Yanukovych's backtracking on a trade agreement with the EU in November 2013 - favouring closer economic relationship with Russia - led to three months of long, escalating protests which were mainly situated in Kiev but were also active in western Ukraine. The government tried to suppress the protests, leaving many dead and injured on both sides. After three months of protests Yanukovich fled to Russia and an interim government set new elections for 25th May 2014. Shortly after Yanukovich's departure, pro-Russian separatists ,who were anonymous Russian soldiers, invaded the Ukraine border claiming to protect Russians and seized official buildings and military bases, especially the important naval base of Sevastopol (Motyl, 2014). Despite protests by the Ukrainian Government, the European Union (EU), the United States of America (USA) and the United Nations (UN) Assembly, Crimea was integrated into the Russian Federation in March 2014. The Ukrainian Government declared Crimea as occupied by Russia but insisted on being the legal owner of the peninsula. Contemporaneous to the Crimean action, pro-Russian separatists occupied parts of the regions of Donetsk, Lugansk and Kharkiv (see map).

Fig. B: Map of regions under control of pro-Russian and Russian forces (red). (The author's own compilation based on the map from Your-Vector-Map.com and the National Security and Defense Council of Ukraine from 23.10.2014)

These regions gained international attention as Ukrainian forces and separatist forces were involved in serious armed conflicts. A new anti-climax was reached after separatists took down an international commercial airplane, namely the Boing 777 from Malaysia Airlines flight MH-17 in July 2014 where 283 people were killed (Basora & Fisher, 2014).

According to the UN Office for the Coordination of Humanitarian Affairs (OCHA) at least 3,707 people were killed and 9,075 people were injured since the beginning of the conflict on 21st November 2013. UN OCHA also counted 415,078 people who were internally displaced and 427,004 who fled to neighbouring countries by 17th October 2014 (UN OCHA, 2014). Furthermore, OCHA estimates these numbers to be even higher than what was originally thought.

The Conflict Parties

Many parties were involved since the beginning of the conflict on 21st November 2013. First the old Ukrainian Government with its President Viktor Yanukovych, who had to give up his position on 22 February 2014 because of ongoing protests from the opposition as well as increased political pressure about the abuse of power and violation of human rights during the demonstration period. The opposition, also called *Euromaidan*, was formed by ten-thousand of pro-European Ukrainians on the independence square *Maidan Nezalezhnosti* in Kiev. The people and one of their most prominent leaders, world-champion boxer Vladimir Klitschko, were demonstrating for their hope of a better European future and against a struggling economy, corruption of the government and Yanukovych's balking to sign a trade agreement with the EU. Klitschko said in a speech on Maidan on 29 November 2013: "Today they stole our dream, our dream of living in a normal country. The failure to sign the agreement of association is treason" (Legge, 2013). Both parties started the conflict but they are a matter of secondary importance in the ongoing conflict.

The core conflict consists of the different desires of the many interested factions. First of these is the new Ukrainian Government under President Petro Poroschenko, who was elected on 25 May 2014 and who wants to secure the integrity of the Ukrainian territory. Next are the pro-Russian separatists who are holding parts of the regions of Donetsk, Lugansk and Kharkiv with armed forces and want to split off from Ukraine. A third party is the Russian Federation with its President Vladimir Putin who support pro-Russian separatists by providing them with weapons, training and political backup, the annexation of Crimea and visas for Russia. On another side of the conflict is the EU with its representatives, which may bail out the Ukrainian state for its gas-bills, and which has interests to integrate Ukraine into the EU. Last but not least is the USA under president Barack Obama who became involved after Russia stepped into the happenings, reintroducing the realists theory of *Balance of Power* (Fortmann, Paul, & Wirtz, 2004).

Ukraine Government versus pro-Russian Separatists

The conflict between the new Ukraine Government and pro-Russian separatists can be simplified with a long on-going division between Ukraine's East (pro-Russian) and West (pro-European), which has its roots at least 20 years ago after the downfall of the USSR. Before this period the people were united as Soviets, but after the fall of the USSR the government and its elites did not manage to reunite the Ukrainian folk, nor did they succeed in establishing a comprehensive Ukrainian nationality or find a consistent path for the European/Russian question (Prokop, 2014). The path of Ukraine's EU integration was decided by the election of Petro Poroschenko for President on 25 May 2014 and pro-EU parties which were the driving force in the government on 26 October 2014. The addition of ballots from Yatsenyuk's People's Front and the Poroshenko Bloc cemented the pro-European trend (nearly 45%). The government's goal is to regain sovereignty and to reunite the apostatised regions, leading Ukraine and the Ukrainian people toward a European future. The separatists, on the other hand, are trying hard to affiliate with Putin's Russia by reasoning that they have nothing in common with a Ukrainian State - in fact separatists feel more Russian or even Soviet than Ukrainian (Hrytsak, 1998). Since 5 September 2014 there has been a ceasefire in place but it tends to be violated daily.

The Russian Federation versus Ukraine

With the deployment of unmarked Russian soldiers to Crimea and support of pro-Russian separatists near the Russian border, as well as the seizing of Ukraine warships, bases and other war equipment, Russia has intervened into the conflict unilaterally. The explanation of the origins of this action can be traced back to past political happenings in NATO and EU, as well as the promotion of democracy in the Ukraine together with sensitive military developments in the border region of Russia (Mearsheimer, 2014) as well as in the Eurasian Economic Union (EEU). First the North Atlantic Treaty Organisation has expanded over the last 20 years eastwards (e.g. Czech Republic, Poland, Bulgaria, Latvia, Estonia etc.) leaving just a few former USSR parts left out (e.g. Ukraine, Belarus etc.). Nearly the same development can be observed concerning the EU, but they are now targeting the Ukraine as well. To sum up: Russia is facing two growing hostile confederations that are coming closer and closer to Russia's border. Furthermore, the USA has founded the National Endowment for Democracy accumulating more than $5 billion since 1991 and hereby has supported over 60 projects to democratise Ukraine, a state at the doorstep to Russia. The naval harbour of Sevastopol is crucial for Russia's access to the Black Sea and crucial to maintain the Black Sea Fleet with around 15,000 personnel and around 50 warships and vessels (Yuhas & Jalabi, 2014). Last but not least there is the EEU which comes into effect on 1 January 2015 as a common customs union for Russia, Belarus and Kazakhstan. Ukraine would be Russia's big coup in the EEU. Without Ukraine the EEU looks increasingly threadbare, Ukraine's population is 10 million more than the combined populations of Armenia, Belarus, Kyrgyzstan and Kazakhstan together (Brooke, 2014). In addition to that Ukraine is a very important defensive trade partner. Ukraine's defence industry exports Antonov Mi 8-17 and Mi-26, helicopter engines and other defence products in a total worth of $1.3 billion not to mention that more than the half of Russia's nuclear arsenal was built in Ukraine (Chroursina & Gomez, 2014).

These preconditions show that it was unacceptable for Russia to stand powerless on the side of the conflict, seeing Ukraine turning westwards and leaving its influence to evanesce. Russia's action is also a deterring measure for the stability of other eastern states (e.g. Belarus) and a clear statement that protests are not tolerated.

The EU, USA and other international countries versus the Russian Federation

As a reaction to Russia's annexation of Crimea and its attempts to influence and to destabilise Ukraine the USA, EU and other countries have imposed three rounds of sanctions on Russia. However these sanctions are not targeting Russia's strong gas exports, because of Europe's and Ukraine's high dependence on Russian gas, but are targeting instead defence companies, banks, and individuals as well as technology used for exploration or production of oil (Department of State, 2014). Russia, on the other hand, decided to impose sanctions against American and Canadian citizens as well as a one year import embargo for agriculture products (Walker & Rankin, 2014). The current situation seems frozen, but the EU and US stated that their sanctions could be removed if the current peace process holds on (Kahn, 2014).

However, the whole conflict is at an escalation phase which is solidified by Putin's speech on 24 October 2014 blaming the USA for its "unilateral diktat" (Anishchuk, 2014). Putin claims not to be responsible for the crisis in the Ukraine. In contrary US President Barack Obama has a different view on the happenings. He stated one month earlier at the UN General Assembly (24 September 2014) that not "might makes right" but "right makes right" indicating Russia's unlawful annexation, supporting of separatists and moving of troops over the Ukraine border (Obama, 2014).

Peace Making Activities

The first steps towards peace were made with new free and fair elections in May and October 2014, therefore ending demonstrations and the standstill. The elections can be seen as a necessary foundation for a democratic peace process and the only chance of reuniting the Ukrainian folk. The new Ukrainian government faces big tasks as it has to solve the division in the country including the conflict with pro-Russian separatists. Also, they must find a way out of the economic crisis, determine a consistent and long-lasting European path, fight corruption and establish human rights, democracy and political participation for every Ukrainian.

One big step to a solution of the conflict would be continuing the ceasefire and having bilateral talks with Russia. At the UN Generally Assembly Prime Minister Arseniy Yatsenyuk has affirmed that out of his sight the origin of the conflict is Russia's invasion, and it is therefore important that in Russia withdraws from the occupied regions and fulfils the Minsk Memorandum from 5 September 2014 (Yatsenyuk, 2014). The Memorandum consists of 12 points including a ceasefire, ensuring, monitoring and verification of the ceasefire by the Organisation for Security and Co-operation in Europe (OSCE) (OSCE, 2014), releasing of hostages and illegal obtained persons and the withdrawing of illegal troops (Ukraine, Russian Federation, DPR, & LPR, 2014). Another mediator in the region is the OSCE which has to manage a complicated task namely to maintain total neutrality to gain both parties trust with its background as a European organisation.

Future Development

Russia exhibits politics of power and territory without concern for international agreements and institutions and therefore was not included in the Group of Eight meetings and is being sanctioned by many international states (see also Gowan, 2014). It is likely to occur that Russia will reduce its efforts in international institutions, driving a wedge between itself and the international community. The question is not only how to make peace in the Ukraine conflict, but also about how not to end up in a new Cold-War which could also affect the balance of existing alliances like the North Atlantic Treaty Organisation.

Bibliography

Anishchuk, A. (2014). Putin accuses United States of damaging world order. Retrieved 25.10.2014, from http://www.reuters.com/article/2014/10/24/us-russia-putin-idUSKCN0ID1A220141024

Auswärtiges Amt. (2014). Länderinformation: Ukraine. Retrieved 23.10.2014, from http://www.auswaertiges-amt.de/DE/Aussenpolitik/Laender/Laenderinfos/01-Nodes_Uebersichtsseiten/Ukraine_node.html

Basora, A. A., & Fisher, A. (2014, 31.07.2014). Ukraine Crisis Timeline: Talk of Peace, Acts of War. Retrieved 22.10.2014, from http://www.fpri.org/geopoliticus/2014/07/ukraine-crisis-timeline-talk-peace-acts-war

Brooke, J. (2014). Putin Kicks Off Eurasian Union, Without Ukraine. Retrieved 25.10.2014, from http://www.voanews.com/content/russia-belarus-kazakhstan-agree-to-create-economic-union/1924941.html

Chroursina, K., & Gomez, J. M. (2014, 07.05.2014). Ukraine's Arms Industry is Both Prize and Problem for Putin. Retrieved 24.10.2014, from http://www.bloomberg.com/news/2014-05-07/putin-eyes-ukrainian-arms-prize-as-troops-build-up-along-border.html

CIA. (2014, 23.06.2014). The World Factbook - Ukraine. Retrieved 22.10.2014, from https://www.cia.gov/library/publications/the-world-factbook/geos/up.html

Fortmann, M., Paul, T. V., & Wirtz, J. J. (2004). Balance of power : theory and practice in the 21st century. Stanford, California: Standford University Press.

Gowan, R. (2014). Now is Not the Time for a 'Grand Bargain' With Russia. World Politics Review. Retrieved 26.10.2014, from http://www.worldpoliticsreview.com/articles/14141/now-is-not-the-time-for-a-grand-bargain-with-russia

Hrytsak, Y. (1998). National Identities in Post-Soviet Ukraine: The Case of Lviv and Donetsk. Harvard Ukrainian Studies, 22, Culture and Nations of Central and Eastern Europe, 263-281.

Kahn, R. (2014, 15.09.2014). New Energy for Russian Sanctions. Retrieved 22.10.2014, from http://blogs.cfr.org/kahn/2014/09/15/new-energy-for-russian-sanctions/

Legge, J. (2013). Ukraine protests: Violent police crackdown to break up pro-Europe demo. The Independent. Retrieved 24.10.2014, from http://www.independent.co.uk/news/world/europe/ukraine-protests-violent-police-crackdown-to-break-up-proeurope-demo-8974649.html

Mearsheimer, J. J. (2014). Why the Ukraine Crisis Is the West's Fault. Foreign Affairs, 9(September/October 2014).

Motyl, A. J. (2014). How far will Putin go? Retrieved 22.10.2014, 2014, from http://www.foreignpolicy.com/articles/2014/03/01/putin_russia_ukraine_intervention_war

Obama, B. (2014). Remarks by President Obama in Address to the United Nations General Assembly. The White House - Office of Press Secretary Retrieved from http://www.whitehouse.gov/the-press-office/2014/09/24/remarks-president-obama-address-united-nations-general-assembly.

OSCE. (2014). OSCE Monitoring Mission to Ukraine: The Facts. Retrieved 27.10.2014, from http://www.osce.org/ukraine-smm/116879?download=true

Prokop, M. (2014, 31.05.2014). Where Does Ukraine's Separatism Come From? Retrieved 24.10.2014, from http://www.neweasterneurope.eu/interviews/1235-where-does-ukraine-s-separatism-come-from

Ukraine, Russian Federation, DPR, & LPR. (2014). 12 Point Memorandum. Minsk: Retrieved from http://www.osce.org/ru/home/123258?download=true.

UN OCHA. (2014). Ukraine Situation Report No.16 as of 17 October 2014. Retrieved from http://reliefweb.int/sites/reliefweb.int/files/resources/Sitrep%2016%20-%20Ukraine.pdf.

Yatsenyuk, A. (2014). Speech in front of the UN Generally Assembly. Retrieved 25.10.2014, from http://www.osce.org/home/123257

Your-Vector-Maps.com (Cartographer). (2012). Map of Ukraine. Retrieved from http://www.your-vector-maps.com/countries/-ukraine/-ukraine-free-vector-map/?image=ukraine

Yuhas, A., & Jalabi, R. (2014). Ukraine crisis: why Russia sees Crimea as its naval stronghold. Retrieved 24.10.2014, from http://www.theguardian.com/world/2014/mar/07/ukraine-russia-crimea-naval-base-tatars-explainer

YOUR KNOWLEDGE HAS VALUE

- We will publish your bachelor's and master's thesis, essays and papers

- Your own eBook and book - sold worldwide in all relevant shops

- Earn money with each sale

Upload your text at www.GRIN.com and publish for free